We
Really
Do
Need
Each
Other

We Really Do Need Each Other

Reuben Welch

Zondervan Publishing House
Grand Rapids, Michigan

WE REALLY DO NEED EACH OTHER
Copyright © 1973 by Impact Books
A Division of John T. Benson Publishing Company

Copyright assigned to The Zondervan Corporation 1982

Zondervan Publishing House
1415 Lake Drive, S.E.,
Grand Rapids, Michigan 49506

Library of Congress Cataloging in Publication Data

Welch, Reuben.
    We really do need each other.

    Reprint. Originally published, Nashville : Impact
Books, [1973]
        1. God—Love—Meditations.   2. God—Worship and love
—Meditations.   3. Love (Theology)—Meditations.
4. Bible. N.T. John, 1st—Meditations.   5. Fellowship—Religious
aspects—Christianity—Meditations.
I. Title.
[BT140.W44 1982]   242′.5   82-20140
ISBN 0-310-70221-6

Printed in the United States of America

86   87   88 — 20   19   18   17   16   15

Contents

Dedication

To Mary Jo—
  With whom for twenty-seven years
  I have shared the joys of being together.
  And I have learned the lesson that togetherness
    means that we really do need each other.

Chapter One

A PLACE TO MEET

I myself am on my own journey.
I don't come to you out of a vacuum.
              I'm in the process of my own pilgrimage.
And I know that you don't come out of a vacuum either—
        that you are on your journey.
And what I believe with all my heart is that in
                  the grace and mercy of God,
               our providential meeting together
can be God's time for some new and fresh thing.
I'm writing to you about the things that I believe
        the most and the best in the whole world.
I want you to know I'm writing about some of the greatest
             stuff in the whole world.
And if I knew anything better to write about
        I would write about it.
I want to tell you that I believe what I am writing to you
      and I'm concerned that you believe it.
   But whether you do or not,
I want you to know that what I am writing to you
        I really believe with all my heart.

What I am sharing with you is both old and new.
It is old in that it is the word of the Bible
              and has been true for a long time.
It is new because the old truth
      has met me in the context of my personal journey
      and is changing my life.

For about a dozen years
I've been a teacher
at a Christian college in California—
for the last five, I've been a college chaplain.
I used to teach Greek—
please be impressed—
and every year we translated First John.
Whether or not it changed many students,
somewhere along the way
it began to change me
and I began to see words like life
and light
and love—
especially love.
And I began to feel John's concern
for the Christian fellowship,
and I began to understand his teaching
that in Christ we belong together
and we really do need each other.

Then I became chaplain of the college—
and the book came alive
as I experienced the living needs
of a living community
not too different
from the one John knew in Ephesus.
I discovered that you don't produce community
by bringing X number of warm bodies
together
and running them through registration.
What a surprise to learn that
compulsory chapel attendance
does not automatically make us
"one in the Spirit"
and "one in the Lord".

From the outside
                    it would seem that
        a Christian college campus would be
                    a sort of an anteroom to heaven—
                                all these students
                    in a similar age group
                with similar religious backgrounds
                and similar socio-economic status,
and interested in Christian higher education
                                    and all wise—
                        especially the sophomores.
But I have found out,
            that in the midst of all these
                        likenesses and similarities,
there can be fragmentation
                    division,
                insecurity,
            and loneliness—

                        mostly
                        loneliness.
I also discovered that what John talked about was true,
    not only for some special group
        somewhere a long time ago—
    it is all about real needs
                of real people like you and me
and it is true for us right where we are.

            I remember when we got concerned at school
about the possibility of a campus becoming ingrown
            and out of touch with the real live world.
        So in an effort to overcome our ingrownness,
we began to have dialogues

                        on race relations,
                        war and peace,
                        Vietnam, the draft,
                    sociological problems,
                                    etc.

So we had our panels and dialogues
and special speakers
and exposed ourselves to the wide world
and somewhere along in the midst
of the whole business
one of our students
tried
to commit
suicide.
I will never recover from that shock.
But here we were—
do you know what we said?
"We are the protected, sheltered
sub-culture
out-of-touch.
We live in a little hothouse
and out there are the real problems
and the real issues of the world.
We cannot do this.
We must expose ourselves."
And somebody right in the midst of us was about to
die.
While we considered the *real* issues of life.

Now I've been thinking a lot about that
and that is why I believe all the issues of life
and death
are present between you and me.
Despair, loneliness, guilt, frustrations
disillusionment, hate, bitterness,
love—you name it.
You name a human emotion—
a human experience—
and it is here between you and me.
We need not talk about some other world.
So let's not think about "out there."
Let's think about "us"
and where we are
and what God wants to say to us now.

I hope you will forgive me
        for being too autobiographical but
                I'm writing about the changing things
            that have been happening to me
since the truth of First John has confronted
                the life situation in my world.
                You will end up knowing me
                        better than I know you—
    and I wish it didn't have to be that way.
Since I am a teacher,
                I am going to give you an assignment.
            If I give you an assignment I'll feel at home
                            and if you don't do it
                    I'll feel more at home than ever.
I would like for you to read First John
            two or three times
                        as you read this book.
Let's just pause here for a moment now and pray as we go.

Lord, here's the Word before us.
                What do you want to say to us from It?
                What do you want to say to me?
                    If we know our hearts
            we are not so much interested in what men
                            can say,
    but we really are interested in what You want to say
                            today.

Father, talk to us
            and say to us
                    what we need
                        to hear from the Word.
                            In Thy name
                    we pray—
                        Amen.

Chapter Two

JESUS BRINGS THE LIFE OF GOD

Who is this Person in our world?; No gap; It's Jesus and me; Me and my and my inner life; Images of oneness.

That which was from the beginning
  which we have heard
  which we have looked upon
              and touched with our hands
                  concerning the word of life—
the life was made manifest
          and we saw it
          and we testify to it
          and proclaim to you the eternal life
  which was with the Father
  and was made manifest to us—
                              that which
                  we have seen and heard
                  we proclaimed also to you
    so that you may have fellowship with us;
and our fellowship is with the Father and
                  with His Son Jesus Christ.
And we are writing this that our joy might be
                      complete.
                          (1 John 1:1-4)

In this first paragraph of First John
          some great realities emerge.
The New English Bible has put a title on First John—
      it is "Recall To Fundamentals"—
and in this first paragraph of chapter one
          two of them stand out—
      "manifested life"
                  and "fellowship."

The "manifested life" of God in Jesus constitutes,
                                        or brings together,
          a "fellowship" of those who share his life
                    in which is found
                              the fullness of joy.
                                        Come to think of it,
              that's what the first section of this book is about.
        In case you don't read it all, you can at least
                                        underline that last sentence.
It's going to take me awhile to write about it.

In terms of fundamentals
              the first one is very clear—
              God's life
                    is manifested to us in Jesus.
Is it really true that God's eternal life
      has come into our world
            at the level where it can be seen
                                        and touched
                                        and heard
                                        and felt
                                        and experienced
                                        and known?
                    Is that really true?
      Is it true that the eternal life of God
has entered into our human situation
                    fully
                    totally
                    utterly?

                                        If it is,
                              it is the best word
        that our earthbound, sinbound hearts have ever heard.
We all know the world has been touched by evil.
        But we must also believe that it
      has been touched by the life of God.
I really do believe this—
I really do.

God's eternal life has come to us
                              right where we are—
                    that's right where you are
                    and that's right where I am.
Did you know that where you are now,
        feeling what you are feeling now,
              thinking what you are thinking now,
Jesus Christ brings to you the very life of God—
                not by some magic stroke of omnipotence—
        but by himself entering into our humanity
bringing with him the very life of God.

                              God's life released
                                  in my world?
                              Yes,
                                  Yes,
                                      Yes.

                              Sometimes at school
                              I have the "privilege"
of teaching an upper divisional general ed. course
        with the profound title of
"Great Movements and Ideas Of Christianity."
It's kind of a poor man's history of Christian thought—
        one quarter,
              thirty pages of outside reading,
                    and a 200-word term paper.
                    It's one of those kinda neat courses.
                              We talk about
                                  God, Man,
                                      the universe—
                    past, present, and future.
We pick up from the time of the early church
        some of the great ideas and movements
that have been involved in the Christian faith.

We start off with the early church fathers—
                                    you know,
the disciples of the disciples of the disciples—
                        in the period of the church
            when they hammered out the great creeds,
            like the Nicene Creed
        and the Chalcedonian Creed—
            aren't you impressed that I know these?—
when they hammered out the great stuff
    that finds its expression
        in the Apostle's Creed
            and in our creeds
                that we hardly ever read
                        or think much about.

You may find this hard to believe
but sometimes, when I am haranguing the students
  in a most exciting way
    about these fantastically interesting subjects
    I get a kind of a radar feed-back from out there
    that carries with it the feeling of SO WHAT?
So we have to stop awhile
    and talk about the SO WHAT.
I don't think we would express the Creeds
            the same way they did
                    if we had to write them again,
but I believe this—
they were dealing with the real thing.

There are two fundamental issues
            that the early church hassled with
                    as it formulated its creeds.

One was—
Is Jesus really
     God among us?
     Is it really God who
     meets us in Jesus?
     What about Jesus?

                 We would say
                    it this way—
     "Is He really divine?"
Of course, we say yes, but that is
       a fundamental question.
You see, here we are
     earthbound, sinbound—
    we know something of our own human existence—
Jesus comes into our world
    and all the creeds that ever were
      are the effort to explain this question:
       what's going on here with this person
             in our world?
Is He in fact God among us?

         Is He almost God,
           nearly God,
            like God,
        something like God?
     Is He the finest flower that ever grew
     in the human garden?
     Is He the greatest person who ever lived
     or
     is He God
        who comes to us?
The creeds say that it is indeed
       God's life that comes.
It isn't just my life magnified,
    or my life purified,
 but it is God's life
     come into my world.

The other issue with which they struggled is this—
Does the life that comes to us from God
really come all the way?
In common terms, the question is—
"Is Jesus really human?"
That's fundamental, isn't it?
Here we are—
earthbound, sinbound.
Is it God's life that comes?
Yes.

Does that life really come,
does it nearly come,
almost come,
or does Jesus enter
fully and totally into our human situation?

I think we believe in the humanity of Christ—
but not really.
I think you think
you believe in the humanity of Jesus—
but I don't think you really do.
And if we would talk about it awhile,
you'd get nervous.
I could write a long time about the divinity of Christ
and you might nod your head and
slowly go to sleep about it,
but when we begin to think about the real humanity
of Jesus

we get nervous—
we are afraid of it.
I don't know why.
Well yes, I guess I do.
We can safely think about the divinity,
but when we think about the humanity
that gets close to where we are
and then when we think about that
we get a little bit spooked.

I think we can put it this way—
                although I'm not sure the creed writers
                        would have said it this way—
        between Jesus and God
                    there is no gap.
        The other half of that is not so easy
                        for people like you and me—
        between Jesus and me
                    there is no gap.
                    Of course, we look up to Him,
but in a deep and wonderful sense—
        we don't look up to Him—
        we look straight across at Him.
            Not because we are exalted
but because He has come down all the way to meet us
flesh of our flesh
                bone of our bone
                    humanity to humanity
                        eyeball to eyeball.

What good is it if Jesus comes to us
but He really doesn't come from God?
            And what good is it if He comes from God
                        but He doesn't really
                            come all the way?
            He is as much one with us
                    in our humanity,
        as He is one with the Father
                in His divinity.

Now when this begins to get hold of us
            we can begin to see that Jesus comes to us,
            not in the exaltation of our humanity,
            but in the depths of our human need.
Do you think we can believe that Jesus comes to us
            in our times of deepest need,
                as we are at our worst?

What this means is
    that into your world
        your context
        your lifestyle—
            I mean just like it is,
            just exactly like it is—
Jesus comes all the way
    and He brings with Him
    the very life of God.
And so there's the hope for my world
        and your world
    and our great big wide world.
If I could always believe it as much as I do
    when I am writing it,
and if you could believe it as much as you do
    when you're reading it,
what a wonderful difference it would make.
                He doesn't say
                "I'm up here.
                Reach up.
                Come up.
                Shape up.
                Get with it.
                Do right
and I'll meet you somewhere in between."
He comes from God—
        bringing God's life—
           "manifested life"—
               to where you are
                  as you are,
                what you are,
                    now.

The second of the great realities
about which John writes is "fellowship."
In that wonderful word "fellowship"
John includes the whole idea
of God's saving purposes
His salvation history
and redemptive deeds.
Let's look at the passage again.
The life was made manifest,
and we saw it,
and testify to it,
and proclaim to you the eternal life
which was with the Father
and was made manifest to us—

that which
we proclaim also to you
so that you may have fellowship with us.

(1 John 1:2,3)

Is he saying that all the reality
of God's manifested life—
that the great truth of the incarnation
is funneled down into fellowship?
Pre-cise-ly.
That's just exactly what he says.
I believe with all my heart
that the bringing of His life creates fellowship.
That which
we have seen and heard
we proclaim also to you
so that you may have fellowship with us;
and our fellowship is with the Father and
with His Son Jesus Christ.

(1 John 1:3)

Fellowship!
See—yours with us and
ours with Him
through His Son Jesus Christ.

Now let's think a little bit
             about that word "fellowship."
I have to tell you that I am at a place
             in my own journey where
             that word is very,
                          very important
        and I'm going to write about it longer
                          than I should,
but not as long as I want to—by a long shot.
What an important word that is
        and I do speak to you out of the context
             of my own life.
                          You see, I have come to believe
                                       with all my heart
                          that the life that Jesus brings
                                       is a shared life.
The life of God in the world
             does not have its meaning in isolated units,
             but in a fellowship of those
                          who share that life in Him.

The word "fellowship" in Greek is "koinonia."
                          You know, Sunday School
                          classes are named that.
                          It means to have a share
                          a sharing together
                          a common participation
             a partaking together
        a having in common.
                  Now as it is used in the New Testament
                          it is a distinctly Christian word.
It has other uses and meanings—
                          for instance,
        Peter and John had koinonia in the fishing business,
                          they had a shared partnership.
        What brought them together was their
        common sharing of the life of fishermen.

The point is—
Christians are not brought together
          because they like each other,
     but because they share a common life in Jesus
                         and are faced with the task
                    of learning how to love each other
                              as members of the family.
I'm sure you could not believe there is ever
               any tension in our home.
There are four of us who live there.
          We have three children—
                    two at home.
          We don't live there
               at our house
          because we just met on the street one day
          and decided we liked each other
                                   and decided
                         to take up living together.
We live together because we are a family,
               and sometimes in the midst of the strife
                         and tension and stress
          what holds us together
          is not the happy fellowship and congeniality
                    but the fact that we are a family.
                         And because we are,
               we're faced with the continual task
                    of learning what love means.
What brings us together is not
          our mutualities and congenialities
               and common interests and hobbies.
               It is not our mutual esteem
                    nor our happy hormones—
          it is our blood ties,
               our common name
               and our common commitment—
     it's our parentage,
       and our heritage
          and our bloodline
               and our life.

And I think that is apt for the church.
So often we say
    "You ought to come to our church—
                        you'd like us.
You'd like our preacher
    you'd like our music
        you'd like our youth program
            you'd like our golden agers
                our fifty-plusers—
                    you'd like us.
              Come, please come
                  do come
              you'd like us."
And if they come—
      and like us
      then well and good.
      But if they don't like us—
          they spin off
          and we say, "Oh, too bad.
They just never did seem to fit in, did they?"
But you see, the church
is not the society of the congenial—
          it is a fellowship
              based on common life in Jesus.
                      It is the will of God
that the Christian life be lived in the context of a
      fellowship of the shared life.
        When I read that back it really
        doesn't seem so profound—
but that really has been changing me.
          I am at a time of emphasis
              upon the fact
              that God has made us in such a way
              that we really do
                  need each other—
and maybe I am reacting against
      what seems to me to be
an over-emphasis on individualism
      in evangelical Christianity.

Some of us are so westernized
    and individualized
    and evangelicalized
             that we have forgotten
             how much we really
             need each other.
I think people like you and me are grossly
                   over-individualized.
I think we have talked about personal salvation
             and individual salvation
             and "me" and "my"
             and "my inner life"
until we have almost isolated ourselves.
And so
we just get the idea that
    it's my life
  and God's life
       and you have your relationship to God
         and I have my relationship to God
       and of course we ought to
       be nice to each other
           and love each other,
      but what really counts is
           "my relationship to God."
                We Christians act
           as though we are deep sea divers.
Here we are in the murky waters of sin—
  but we have the protection of the diving suit of God
                     and
             we have the lifeline
      that goes to the great white ship up above.
You have your life in Christ
           and your lifeline
and I have my life in Christ
           and my lifeline
        and here we are with all our lifelines
              going up.

And we say to each other
  "How's your lifeline brother,
    you got any kinks?
      Get it straightened out,
        keep the oxygen going
          or the murky waters of sin
                    will come rushing
                              in on you."
  We wave to each other
and write notes to each other
    and we bump each other around
  and we say to each other—
                  "Get your lifeline
                            right."
                    But here I am
                    all by myself.
      Once in awhile someone gets the bends
      and we bump him up to the top
      or just cut him off
                  and let him
                  drown.
                  That's not the way it is—
              because our life that we have with God
                is not just my life and His—
                    no way.
I know this vertical relationship is fundamental.
I know that what constitutes us a community
              is His life given.
      I'm not saying
          that our relationship to God
              is not personal and unique.
                I'm saying that we are over-
                      individualized.
      You know what I'm doing
      I'm over-exaggerating—
      but not very much.

The
vert-
ical
line
of
God-
ward
rela-
tion-
ship
and the horizontal line of human relationship
are not two lines but one line in a continuum.
It all belongs together.
I'm not talking about what ought to be
  or what would be nice if it were—
    I'm talking about God's reality
      about the way He has constituted
        the life we have with Him.
Our life with Him is tied to,
      is one with
      our life with our brothers
        and sisters.

Like the old hymn says—
    "You can't have one without the other."

There are a couple of ideas
  going around in my mind here
    and one of them is this isolation thing—
    this over-individualization that we have.
When we feel like we are slipping spiritually
    or growing cold
    or indifferent
we have a tendency to withdraw and pray through
    or to get hold of God
    or get back to where we ought
      to be
    so we will have something to give
      to others—
    and that's false.

That separates the full and the empty
            the haves and the have-nots—
        we are all have-nots,
        we are all emptys.
Somebody said, "Real witnessing is
        one beggar
        telling another beggar
                where to get bread."
                        We are all beggars—
        we don't have anything but the life of Christ
and his life in us is not separate
                    from our life with
                        each other.

And I think we are helped in this feeling of isolation
        by the songs that we sing.
                I'm thinking of the old song,
        "On the Jericho Road,
                there's room for just two
no more and no less
                just Jesus and you."
                    And I remember the chorus—
        "Now it's just Jesus and me."
I live at school you know
    and I think the only time
        that song is appropriate
            is on a Friday night in the dorm
                when everybody else
                    is on a date.
                    Then that's a good time to sing,
                "Jesus and me."
Here's another:
        "When I am burdened
            or weary or sad
        Jesus is all I need"
or:
        "Are you weary,
            are you heavy-hearted
        tell it to Jesus alone."

Of course there is truth in all these songs.
Of course we believe in the total adequacy
of Jesus Christ
to meet the total need of
the total person.
But we must remember this also—
He saves in the context of the community of faith.
It isn't "Jesus and me"
it is "Jesus and we"
and on the Jericho Road
there is room for Jesus
and the whole redeemed
community.
And if you are like me,
when you are
burdened and weary and sad
you need Jesus but you also need
someone to be Jesus to you—
someone to bring His healing presence to you.
And sometimes the answer to your weariness
and heavy-heartedness
is not to "tell it to Jesus alone"
but to begin to share
and care with someone else.
You can get yourself in a little spiral of self-pity
and so you tell it to Jesus alone
and increase your self-pity
and your martyr complex.
"Lord, I'm so persecuted.
but Lord you understand."
Way to go.
That's enough to bless this dying world, isn't it?
Well, let's go on singing the good songs—
it's okay.
They aren't true, but it's okay.
You see we really do need each other,
not because of the inadequacies of God
but because this is the way His grace works.

I suddenly remember a student at school
who just before he was to graduate
had to go into the hospital with cancer—
                                    and he died.
                            He was twenty-two,
                and he was a ministerial student
and Frank Carver, head of our department, and I
                            were very close to him—
and we went out to see him and had long talks with him
                        about life
                                and death
                                        and God.
He knew what was happening and he said,
                                    "You know,
                I know that God has worked in the past
and I know that God will be with me
                when I cross the river.
            I know He will be there,
                    it is those times in-between
                        that sometimes are rough."
Do you understand that?
Sure you do and so do I.
                        I know God has been with me,
                    I know God will be with me in the crisis,
                            but here I am right now.
He said,
"I just wish I was conscious of His presence at all times,
                                        like now
                            when I need it."
And Frank said to him,
"You know,
        Jesus comes to you
            in the persons who come to you."
                                Now that is true.
                        Have you experienced that?
                                        I have.
It is also true
        that people can bring the devil
                and sometimes we're more familiar
                                with that.

But once in awhile someone comes
                  and brings
                        Jesus to me.
    God has made us this way.
    We really do need each other.

The point of the passage here, I think,
    is that Christians are to recognize this reality.
John was calling them back to the fundamentals
because the fellowship was being threatened,
as it still is.
          How is it healed?
                By coming back to
                the great realities
                that constitute what we are—
                the life that we have
                in Jesus is a shared life.
Early Christians were often together
    around those things
      which made them what they were.
      They often met together to express
        their oneness in Christ—
        around the teaching
        around the Word
        around the sacraments
    and around prayer.
They were being together as Christians
    not just Christians being together,
                I think this is more
                than playing with words.
      There is a fundamental difference between
          the fellowship of Christians
      and Christian fellowship.
Too often we are together as Christians
      doing the things we like to do together—
        volley ball, parties, teas, leagues,
        receptions and what-not.

Or we get together and talk about cars
and sports and babies and clothes
and weather and Sunday School attendance
  and we come away having talked
                  and laughed
                  and enjoyed ourselves;
                          but strangely
                        empty and lonely
                  and a little bit guilty.

It does not deepen
  the oneness of the fellowship
    to multiply such activities.
  These things do not express our oneness
    but the study of the Word does
            the sacraments do
            and prayer does.
We need to be together more
  doing the things that really give expression
    to the common life we share.

You know the best symbol of all this—
    the Lord's Supper.
I have a mental image about the Lord's Supper.
      I see a table in the upper room—
Can you see it?
      Jesus is at the head of the table
      and the disciples around the sides.
  And then I see the wall open up
    and the table begins to lengthen—
      and it lengthens out through
                  the first century
             and the second century
      and it comes all the way into our world
              to where we are.
Jesus is at the head of the table
    and all the believers of all the ages
  are gathered at the table
    and we are one
      at one table
        with the Lord.

What is it that makes us one?
We share that broken,
                             given life
and so we come
and we are one.

There is a beautiful phrase in Galatians 2:9
              that expresses this.
Paul and his company had gone out from Antioch
                              into the Gentile world
and the saints in Jerusalem were insecure
   because the "general board"
        hadn't approved it.
                    But they had gone out on their own
                    and they were coming back
                              somewhat anxiously
                    and the church gave them
                    "the right hand of fellowship."
It meant that across the prejudices
              across the hesitancies
              across the insecurities
              across the normal barriers
                    that would have separated them,
                         they reached out and said,
           "God bless you—
            here is my hand."
And I tell you this—
if somewhere in this world
         there are people who are sharing
                    the life of Jesus together
                    and who are helping each other,
                    and suffering with each other,
                              that's my crowd.
                    Those are the people—
           that is the community
of which my heart yearns to be a part.
And the name of it is the church
                    the body of Christ
                    the fellowship of believers.

Let's pray—
        Lord Jesus,
teach us to know
    that what makes us one
        is our oneness in the Lord.
And don't let us dilute
            or weaken it
            until we become
                a society of the congenial.
                        We would be indeed
                        the body of Christ.
Teach us to know
    how very much we need each other.
    Help us to learn how
    to be sensitive to each other
    and open and accepting of each other.
Thou who has brought the life of God to bring us
                        together—
        may our fellowship be the fellowship
            of the Father
            the Son
                and the Holy Spirit.
                    Amen.

Chapter Three

WALKING IN THE LIGHT OF GOD

God is a good person; Taking the roof off; To say the same; But if.

So Jesus brings the life of God into our world;
    He brings it all the way down
        to where we live.
The life He brings is a shared life,
                    a life that creates a fellowship.
I wish I hadn't already written about this
            because I could write about it
                and write about it
                and write about it.
But there's some more great stuff
                to be said
            about the quality of life
        within this fellowship.
            Now the question that arises is this:
What is to be the quality of life within this fellowship?
What kind of a life is it that is shared by those who are
                            partakers
                    of the life of Christ?
I have come to believe
        that the life we share together in Christ
        is to be a life of openness
                and honesty
            and confession before Him
                in deep recognition of our humanness
                        and weakness
                        and failure.

Let's begin here:

> **This is the message we have heard from Him**
> **and proclaim to you**
> **that God is light**
> **and in Him**
> **is no darkness at all.**
>
> **(1 John 1:5)**

I think that is a major premise.
  I wish you could hang a big sign from the ceiling—
> put it high enough
> because we are going
> to hang some little
> signs beneath it—

  hang it out in front of you
  and print on it these words:

> **God is Light.**

Every once in awhile you can look up from the book
  and see it.
Don't take it down—
  it needs to stay there.
    It's the major premise
      and everything else we are going to say
        hangs on the hooks underneath.

> That's where it begins,
> **God is Light.**

And John adds this phrase—

> **and in Him is no darkness at all.**

In the Greek language they don't mind double negatives.
  We don't use them
but the Greeks did
    and John did it on purpose for emphasis
          and what he really meant is
      that there is no darkness in God—

> no, not at all,
> no darkness . . . at all,
> none,
> no darkness,

      never no how.

Let's think about that for a minute.
The idea of God being light
is not unique to the Christian faith
or to the Judeo-Christian tradition,
but in the Biblical context
it has some specific meanings that
are tremendously significant to us
in relation to our life
in the fellowship of believers.
One of them is—
God is light . . .
and you can trust Him.
God doesn't have any dark folds in His cloak.
There is no deceit
no caprice
no trickery
no hypocrisy
no game-playing with God.
He is light
is true
is pure—
He is sincere.
We don't use that word about God
but He is sincere.
God is a person of integrity—utterly.
He is not hiding anything beneath the folds of His garment.
He is open
is light
is true—
He can be utterly trusted
because He is light.
Now that doesn't say anything that you didn't know already;
but how often we think of God
and talk about Him as though
He were a hidden, deceitful God
with things about Him that you can't really trust
and you better be careful.
But I tell you God is not like that;
God does not play games with us.

Can we believe in the basic integrity of God?
I've talked to people
who talk about God as though when they prayed
they had to say it right
or He wouldn't answer.
Can you hear God saying,
"I want to help but you aren't asking right,
so there's nothing I can do."
And people who think you have to be careful
what you tell God you won't do
because sure as the world
that's just what He'll make you do.
You know, don't tell God you won't go to the jungles
as a missionary—
because He might be up there saying,
"I heard that!
And I've got news for you."
I've talked to people who talk
who think
who believe
that He says,
"You think you know what I want you to do,
but you wait ten years
and when you are way out here
I'm just going to cut you off."
Sometimes we get to feeling that way,
as though we have to penetrate the mystery.
But God is light,
there is no darkness in Him.
He is not trying to trick you.
We are not dealing with darkness—
we are not dealing with subterfuge.
I think I spelled
that big word right!
We are dealing with light.

Maybe I ought not to write about this
    but I think I will anyway.
We've all heard about the invisible deadline . . .
                when you say no to God
                  and no to God
      there's an invisible deadline
          and when you cross over,
            you have had it.
And you don't ever know when you're crossing over
      so you'd better be careful.
          That doesn't compute
          in terms of
          God is Light.
You know, here you are on the path of light
    and you come to the last no—
            usually about the
            fourteenth verse of
            "Almost Persuaded"
        on the last night of fall revival
           and you've had it.
As though God has drawn an invisible line across your path
    and when you cross it
      even though you don't know it
      you have had it.
We know it is dangerous for us to say no to God
      but He will not damn us
        for crossing an unknown line—
        because He is light.
Either that is true
          or it is not true.
    And if God is light
      in Him is no darkness.
If we are going to talk about shadows and darkness
    we're not talking about God
      we're talking about us
      and that is what the rest of the passage
               is about.

That does not mean there is no mystery about God
and His providence—
He is God and we are human.
We are not "on top of" Him to understand His ways—
you can't say I understand mathematics,
English,
and God.
But this we have got to know and believe—
He is a good person,
He is light,
and we can trust Him
totally.

Another Biblical meaning
of the phrase "God is Light" is this:
God is light,
God shines,
light shines!
That's quite profound—
aren't you glad you read this book to find that out?
Light shines!
He is open to us.
He reveals Himself.
The life of God comes to us
as light that shines in Jesus.
The light of God
which is beyond our comprehension
is focused on us in Jesus—
God shines toward us in Jesus.
In Him
we see the brightness of God's glory,
the expressed image of His person.

The pure,
  holy,
    God of integrity
        shines in the life of Jesus Christ.
            Jesus said,
              "I am the light of the world."
In the face of Jesus
  we behold the light of the glory of God.

But what about us?
Here we are in a fellowship
created by the given life of God
            who is light—
            but we are not light.
        He is light but we are not light.
Then what is to be the quality of our lives?
This seems to me
  to be the very issue
    faced in the scriptures that follow.
    Now what we want to do
              is to hang six smaller signs
              down below the big one—
          each of which begins with the word "if."
              They are couplets,
          and they are kind of opposites.
They go like this:
If we say
  we have fellowship with Him
    while we walk in darkness,
      we lie
        and do not live
          according to the truth . . .
                      if we walk
                      in the light
                    as He is in the light
                we have fellowship with one another,
and the blood of Jesus his Son cleanses us from all sin.
                      (1 John 1:6,7)

If we say
  we have no sin
  we deceive ourselves
    and the truth is not in us.

          If we confess our sins,
          He is faithful and just,
          and will forgive our sins
      and cleanse us from all unrighteousness.
              (1 John 1:8,9)

If we say
  we have not sinned,
  we make him a liar
  and his word is not in us.

          If anyone does sin,
        we have an Advocate with the Father,
          Jesus Christ, the Righteous.
           (1 John 1:10, 2:1)

Notice that the first line of each couplet begins with,
        "If we say,"
each one is followed by words that indicate in some way
    a denial,
    or a rejection,
    or an ignoring of our humanness
        our guilt
        our weaknesses
        our failures and our sins.
           "If we say,
           if we say,
           if we say"—
evidently somebody around Ephesus was saying.
        And John is saying,
          "No-no, no."
      Look up at the first one:

If we say
  we have fellowship with Him
    while we walk in darkness,
    we lie,
      and do not live
        according to the truth.

Look,
God is light
   and if we say we have fellowship with Him
while we are still walking in darkness,
      that's not true,
       that is a lie.
God is light—
we cannot say
we have fellowship with light
      and walk in darkness,
       no way.
That's probably what it says in the Greek—no way.
 What does that mean in plain English?
I think it means
 that the quality of our lives
  does make a difference—
   there is no way to say it doesn't matter.
  Don't get to thinking that cutting the corners
     doesn't make any difference—
       it does.

God is light—
 in Him is no darkness.
     If you think a few shadows
      now and then
     don't make any difference—
      that's a lie.
We have lots of ways
 to handle our failures.
  We can rationalize them
    define them,
    ignore them,
   or pretend they don't make any difference—
      but that's not true.
   You can't write them off that way.
God is light—
in Him is no darkness.

Let's look at the second one:
If we say
 we have no sin
 we deceive ourselves
  and the truth is not in us.
We cannot say
  sin does not belong to us.
If we deny the reality of sin in our nature—
                no-no, not me, not us—
if we deny our fundamental sinfulness,
we are only deceiving ourselves
  and turning away from the truth.

                The truth is, you see
we are sinners
  born into the stream
    of a sinful humanity
      and there is no way to deny that
      and keep squared with the truth.

Here is the third one:
If we say
 we have not sinned
 we make Him a liar
  and His word is not in us.
                We aren't supposed to cover up
                      hide or deny,
                    defend or define,
                        or pretend
                that our weakness or failure
                        and sin
                      didn't happen.
We cannot refuse to accept the reality
  of failure in the acts and attitudes
    of our lives.

I know a dear family,
  and once in awhile
the father gets his feelings hurt
                    or is disappointed,
                    or misunderstood—
                    and when that happens—
                    he just clams up.
  Now don't get nervous,
    I'm not talking about you—
      I'm talking about the father.
                    He handled this by total withdrawal
                        from the flow of family life.
    Oh, he said good morning
                pass the potatoes
                and thank you—
                but he really wasn't there.
And then everybody else
  would start walking around softly—
    "pussyfooting it" is the term, I think—
                    trying not to upset Father
                    and trying to keep peace.
  I'm not talking about you, I'm really not.
    Father was miffed
    Mother got a migraine,
    and everyone was paying for it.
    But one fine day
    Father was alright again
    and everything was okay.
                        He had some way
            of communicating this to the family—
                some word,
                some gesture,
                some small gift or conversation
                    would signal the family
                    that he was alright again
and life would come on back to "normal"
  with never a word to indicate
    that anything had ever been other
      than perfectly regular.

The migraine faded,
the tiptoeing ceased
all as though nothing
had ever been different
and the incident was never mentioned—
ever.
You understand that, don't you?
Here is this detour—
undiscussed
unconfessed
unshared
unrecognized
denied
"it didn't happen."
So life now is supposed to go on
until by and by
it would happen again.
And everybody was supposed to pretend
nothing was changed
nothing was different,
everything just like it was,
and God's word says—no.

He is light,
He is truth.

He does not play games with us
and we cannot play games with Him.

Then how are we to respond in terms of our weakness
and failure
and sin?
Perhaps we need a parenthesis here.
The word that is used in this passage
is the word "sin"
but it is the word "sin"
in the broadest sense,
of "missing the mark."
It's "harmartia."

Some groups use the word "sin,"
for anything short of the divine ideal,
whether it is a bad mood in the morning
or shooting your grandmother at night.
And some people
just don't use the word "sin" at all
in connection with Christian people in the church.
You say sin
and they
immediately think of the
bad guys on the outside.

Since it's not easy
to make all those fine distinctions
I would like to put it all together
and use the word "failure."
Maybe then, we won't be so tempted
to pass this section of First John
on to others who need it.
We "all" need it.
I don't think it is right
that there should be
any part of the Bible
about which we can say,
"Oh, I've already finished that exercise—
now let's go on to something else.
I've passed my exam on First John."
I have a feeling that all of the Bible
keeps speaking to all of us
all of the time
and since this passage has something
to say to us,
wherever we are on our spiritual journey,
I'm trying to find a word
that isn't a "red flag" word.
If I would talk to you about "sin"
there would be a kind of a resistance,
but I believe we all know something
about the meaning of "failure"
in our Christian life.

Sometimes when I am speaking on this subject
> *I ask the question,*
"Is there anybody here
> *that doesn't know anything about failure?*
> > *Would you please stand*
> > *and we will pray for you*
> > > *and the other liars."*
> *Alas, I alone am usually left standing.*

John is not speaking
> to any specific group in the church—
> > he is not distinguishing between the "carnal"
> > > and the "spiritual."
He writes to the church and
> to all those in its fellowship.
And through the passage
he speaks to us
> who, on our journey,
> know something of what it means
> > to be human and weak
> and know something about failure.
It speaks to us in the context
> of spirit-filled living
> and of the daily struggle.
> It speaks to every man who will hear it,
> > saint or sinner,
and says something about the quality of life
> within the community of believers.
> > Now, what is that quality of life?

You see, the life that Jesus brings
> is the life of the God who is light.
> In Him is no darkness at all
> > but what
> > about us?
Caught as we are in our humanness,
> our prejudices and weaknesses,
> our failures and our moods,
with all the contingencies of our lives
> in a fallen world—
> > what about us?

What about you and I—
   the people who are a part of the dark world
               into which Jesus came?
        His life has gathered us into a fellowship.
     And I have come to believe with all my heart
     that the passage says,
     that in that fellowship
       we are to live in openness
          and honesty
          and confession
in full and continual awareness
   of the realities of our humanness
    and our weaknesses
    and our failures.
Each of the "if we says" is in some way
       a denying
      or a defending
      or a pretending about our
        real situation
          as
        fallen
        humans.
I'm not saying that the Christian life
  is a perpetual series of failures and guilts
   because that's not true.
But I am reminding us
   that we are human
   and we are weak.
        We are not strong
      we are the have-nots
    and our salvation is by grace.
And all through our journey
  we know the meaning of moods
  and loss of psychic energy.
We know the meaning of failure
and we know the tragedy of broken homes
       and broken relationships
        which we have both received
  and to which we have made our small contribution.

We have been hurt,
          and we have hurt;
               we have been the "tragic-tee,"
          and we have been the "tragic-tor."
We live in a world of broken relationships
     in which we have shared and
     to which we have contributed.
If we are going to talk about fellowship
                    one with another in Him
and the fact that God has created us
                    in the vast complexities
                    of the interpersonal world
then we can't withdraw ourselves
     and have life with God
     and not pick up our share
                         of both the reality
                         and the fallenness
                    of those relationships.
                    We can't do that.

If we start
          the defining, ignoring business
we find ourselves
     moving into darkness
          and lying
               and deceit
                    and the light of God
                    casts its inevitable judgment
                    on our weakness and
                         guilt and
                         failure.

Well, so far
     we have gathered up
          three fundamental truths:
                              God is light
                         we are not light
                    and we can't define,
                              defend,
                              pretend,
                         or ignore it.

Then how are we going to handle our situation?
       Let's look up at the big sign.
Well, thank God, there are three more "if's"
               up there to give us hope.
Look at the second line
       of each of the three couplets.
If we say . . . NO!

                                        But
                              if we walk
                              in the light,
                         as He is in the light
               we have fellowship with one another
        and the blood of Jesus, His Son cleanses us from
                                        all sin.
                              (1 John 1:7)

What does it mean to walk in the light?
 If God is light
        means God shines—
for me to walk in the light
        means for me to walk
                      in the shining of God.
The best way I know to think about that is
God shines in Jesus
   and when I am walking in the light
      I am walking with the roof of my life
         open to the shining of God.
I understand that kind of mental image—
      to walk in the light
      means to take the roof off,
             open up the ceiling
         and let the Son shine in.
                      Now that is the opposite of
                      defining
                      hiding
                      pretending,
                      those are the covers—
         to walk in the light is to take the covers off.
It means exposing my life
                to the verdict of God.

It means all the doors of my life
                         are open to him—
             all the closets
             all the rooms
             and all the cupboards.

And the next "if" clause
     is very much like the first one.
If we say . . . NO!

                    But if we confess our sins,
                         He is faithful and just
                         and will forgive our sins
             and cleanse us from all unrighteousness.
                              (1 John 1:9)

I believe that confession
          and walking in the light
               are Siamese twins.
They belong together in the same way
     that the "if we say" clauses
          belong together.

                    Walking in the light means
                         living in openness and confession.
We've got to let God render verdict
     on the whole—
bringing the whole of life into the presence of God
     so that His light shines
          on every part of it.
What a blessed and awesome thing!
                    I think we ought to put in
                         this marvelous parenthesis:
we must all come under the judgment of God,
               but the judgment of God
                    is such that it is our salvation.

I'm thinking of judgment in the sense
     of letting God render verdict,
     of exposure to the truth of God.
Our salvation is not in deceit
                    or cover-up
                    or hiddenness of our real situation.

It is in the truth
        of the God
            who is light.
The light that reveals
        is the light that cleanses and heals—
                    like opening up
                        the wounds of our life
                to the sunshine of God's love.
The opening of life to God,
                to His judgment,
                that is where
                    we are saved.

That is why we don't get very far
                    defining and explaining
                    our attitudes and behaviors.
"That wasn't really worry—
            that was concern."   *Beautiful.*
"That wasn't anger—
            that was righteous indignation."   *Lovely.*
"That wasn't a lustful look—
            that was an appreciative glance." *Marvelous.*
You see, I know some of these phrases myself.
            We have got to say "OK, Lord.
                    Here it is.
                    You name it."
What is so awful in the covering up is that
                    we go on,
                    unjudged
                    unrebuked
                    unchecked
            and uncleansed.
What I cover up
    I'm left with—
what I open up
        receives not only the revealing of God,
                but also the healing of God.

And that is the growing edge of life
    what He reveals—
        He heals,
    what He illumines—
        He cleanses
             and that is our salvation.
    God's marvelous grace
    meets us right where we are.
If we confess,
He is faithful,
   He is just,
      He will forgive and cleanse.

The word confession is a beautiful word—
             it really means
          "to say the same."
      It means
    "I say what is."
    It is like the old phrase
           "to own up."
              To confess to something is to own it.
      To own up-have you heard that phrase?
What does that mean—
      it means to go ahead and say,
       "That belongs to me."

Maybe this doesn't happen at your house
            but at our house
            my young son will say,
"Can I take my plate
    and go in
        and watch TV?"
So he puts the food in the plate
    then puts the glass on
    then the silverware
          and the napkin
    and starts into the hall
           balancing all of this precariously.

Sure enough,
    halfway down the hall,
        there is this awful crash.
                "What happened?"
                "It fell."

Now my wife has a thing
    about telling the truth.
She always responds "It what?"
        "It fell."
     "All by itself?"
    "No, I did it."
And this happens, too, at my house,
    the family is seated at the table
        and suddenly a glass of milk goes over.
Everyone jumps up and does something
    but the one who spilled it—
        suddenly he is just paralyzed
          "What happened?"
          "It fell."
And the little bit of perversity in Mary Jo says,
     "It what?"
     "It fell."
"Oh, it did, did it?
    What happened?"
        "I knocked it over."
        "Oh."
I really think this is very important
    and not playing with words at all.

    Somebody runs off with somebody
        and a home splits up.
                What happened?
            It was just one of those things—
"Oh, it was, was it?" It just happened—
"Oh, it did, did it?"
Confession says, "I did it"—
    it is the owning of it.
        But you know, this point of owning it
        is the point of the forgiveness of it.

The good news of it is this—
    that God in Jesus Christ forgives all sin—
  tangled-messed up relationships,
    old destructive habit patterns,
      bitterness and resentment.

Let me push this
    in one more direction.
This passage has helped me in my pilgrimage
    to the point that I have made up my mind
    to never go back
      and start over again in the Christian life.

It has helped me understand
    that God's intention for me is
        to keep going on
        and not start over
        at every point of failure.
The point of failure should become
    the occasion for immediate confession
    and trust in the forgiveness
            and cleansing of God.
And it has meant everything for me
        to make up my mind to that.

My daughter, Susan,
plays the piano beautifully—
  though, I must say, not as beautifully as she should
    in the light of all the lessons we have paid for.
When she would get a new piece when she was younger
she would sit down and begin work on it.
She would make it through the first staff
    and about halfway through the second
    and make a mistake.
You already know the next step.
    She would go back and start over—
                louder,
make the same mistake
  at the same place
        and do it again—
            LOUDER!

I've thought a lot about that
 and that's what we do in the Christian life, isn't it?
On the average
  most folk I know have started over
   at least twenty-five times before—
       probably you have, too.
Well, what are you
going to do now?
Do we need to sing "Just As I Am" thirteen times
     or "Almost Persuaded" fourteen times?
I'm not writing about these precious songs
  that the Holy Spirit
   has used in beautiful ways—
I'm writing about
what I believe to be
God's thing for me
    at my point of failure.
I don't need a new
    and louder beginning
       of the Christian commitment.
    I need to open it up
      and let the light shine,
      and then keep going on.
I already know the first five bars
       of the Christian life
        by heart.
     God knows I have played them enough.
     I've made up my mind to finish the song.
I probably couldn't do a perfect performance
      if I did it a hundred times—
  and neither can you.
But whether it is a sin,
    or a blunder,
    or a mistake,
    or a failure,
it has to be handled in the same sort of way—
by opening it up to God
    and walking in the light.

There is one more "if" clause.
It begins with a clear statement
of the divine ideal:
My little children
I am writing this to you
so that you may not sin.
(I John 2:1)

I understand that, don't you?
I know what God's intention is—
I know what is His will
and I know what is the ultimate goal.
It is life without failure and
life without sin.
And it is His promise
that someday we shall be like Him
for we shall see Him
as He is.
(I John 5:2)

But life now is in-between the times—
between the first coming
and the second coming—
and we are caught
here in life between—
between what we were
and what we want
to be.
We know something of the forgiving
cleansing grace of God
and we know something of what it means
to be human
and fallen,
and weak,
and failing.
How beautiful that this last "if" clause
meets us with such profound
and tender understanding
of the flow of our lives in Christ.
His intention is clear.

My little children I am writing this to you
that you sin not . . . but if!
But if anyone does sin
we have an advocate with the Father
Jesus Christ, the Righteous.
We would never have had the courage
to put that in yet how desperately we need it.
Isn't that great?
Let's just put it this way:
My little children
my intention is
that all marriages be happy
and mature
and fulfilling—

but if . . .

My little children
I'm writing this
that all of you be healthy and whole
in body and mind—
but if . . .

I'm writing this
so there won't be brokenness,
tragedies,
scars
but if . . .
Suddenly into the realities of a fallen world
and into the brokenness of it comes this healing word:
we have an advocate.
Not at the point of our achievement,
but at the point of our failure.
Christ the Advocate is by our side,
on our side.
Righteous Jesus Christ
and He is the expiation for our sins—
not our struggles
not our self-hate
not our self-loathing
nor our rash promises or vows—
He is our advocate, our way to handle our sins.

Let's pray together:

Lord Jesus
>   **teach us to know**
>>   **that the quality of life**
>>>   **we are to share—**

is one of openness and honesty and confession.

Teach us to know
>   **the answer to our failures.**
>   **Some of us need to know**
>>>   **that the answer to deep**
>>>>   **guilt and sin**
>>>   **is not to define**
>>>>   **or defend**
>>>>   **or to pretend**

but it is to walk in the light.
>   It is to take the roof off to Thee.

It is to confess
>   to own
>   to open up

in the full assurance that the grace of God
>>   heals
>   and forgives
>>   and cleanses
>   and restores
>>   and renews
>   and that Thou does come to stand
>>   by our side
>   at the point of our failure.

Teach us to live in openness to Thee.

Amen.

Chapter Four

WHAT DOES IT MEAN TO LOVE

Put it down brother; Splangknalevel dialogue;
Love that behaves like Jesus; On becoming a
people people.

Now here is what I have been saying—
you can tell I've been teaching long enough
                              that I "loves" review—
                    Jesus brings to us
                              into our world,
                                   all the way into our world,
                                             the very life of God.
                    And the life He brings is a shared life—
                    and it always creates a community.
                    It isn't Jesus and me,
                    it is Jesus and we.
          We really do need each other.
          God has made us this way.
          The quality of life
               within this fellowship of those
               who share the life of Jesus
                    is to be one of openness
                         and confession
                         and honesty before Him.

          You see,
          Jesus brings the life of the God
                                   who is light.
                    This life we share
                         is to express itself outward
                                   in the community of believers
                                   in terms of love.
                         I want to talk about that love.

Read the Word with me.

For this is the message
  which we have heard from the beginning
    that we should love one another,
                    and not be like Cain,
who was of the evil one and murdered his brother.
              And why did he murder him?
      Because his own deeds were evil
        and his brother's righteous.
      Do not wonder, brethren,
        that the world hates you;
we know that we have passed out of death into life,
    because we love the brethren.
      He who does not love remains in death.
(Pretty strong words, aren't they?)
Anyone who hates his brother is a murderer.
I think he is saying,
  now there are Cain and Abel,
    but let's not talk Cain and Abel,
      let's talk you and me.
      Anyone who hates his brother is a murderer.
      And you know that no murderer
        has eternal life abiding in him.
By this we know love
  that He laid down His life for us,
    and we ought to lay down our lives
      for the brethren.
          (1 John 3:11-18)

                What does it mean to love?
                  Let's take a look.
First of all,
let me share with you
      a couple of words and phrases
        that have come to have real meaning for me.

One of them is the phrase "lay down."
I have had problems with these two words.
 It's easy to understand the
               "he laid down his
                life for me" part
               and that's good, that's okay.
But when it comes to the
               "we ought to lay
                down our lives" part
               that doesn't go too good.
       I mean I love you—
               but I don't want to die for you—
               not before Monday anyway.
And I don't think you want to die for me
  and I'm not sure it would help a whole lot
     even if you did.
  And neither do I think we can explain it by saying
     we must be willing to.
                    In fact,
               as we get older
the things we are willing to die for get fewer
                              and fewer.
       The young can die for all causes.
  But the things I'd die for are very few
and the people I would die for are nearly none at all.
You understand that too,
   because that's true of you as well.
But I have been both helped and challenged by this—
       the word "lay down" means precisely what it says.
I know that in the laying down of His life
    He did in fact give His life.
           But before He died, Jesus "laid down His life."
           The word, "lay down"
               comes from the Greek word which means
                    "to place" or "to put."
                    It means
                    just put it down,
                    lay it down.

Now He just put His life down for us;
we ought to put our lives down for the brethren.
Thankfully that does not mean go out and die,
　　　but it does mean go ahead and just put it down.
I'm not sure what all that means,
　　　but I think I know a little bit about what it means
　　　　　　　　　　　　　　to hold it back
　　　　　　　　　　　　　　And that helps—
　　　　　　　　　　　　　　　and hurts.
Sometimes I wonder what are we saving ourselves for.
Now I don't like this anymore than you do,
　　it's just that I happen to believe
　　　　　that the Bible means what it says
　　　　　　　　　.　about some of these things
　　　　　　　　　even though we don't like them.
　　　I'm thinking of a man
　　　　　　　　　　　　who all his life long saved
　　　　　　　　　　　　　　and saved
　　　　　　　　　　　　　　and saved
　　　　　　　　　　　　　　and held back—
　　　　　　　　　　　　　　　you know—
　　　　　　　　　don't loan and don't borrow
　　　　　　all it brings is trouble and sorrow.
That's the life slogan—don't loan, save, take care—
and all of his life he worked and saved and I guess
　　　　　　　　　　　　　he made it.
And do you know what he did when he was about sixty-
　　　　　　　　　　　　　four?
　　　　　　　　Yeah-he up and died—
　　　　　　　　that's what he did.
　　　　　　　　And all of the saving,
　　　　　　　　keeping, holding, making
　　　　　　　　making, keeping, holding
　　　　　　　　saving of his life—
　　　　　　　　was down the tubes
　　　　　　　　forever.
　　Now I'm not talking about economics.
I'm talking about a lifestyle
　　that seeks to preserve, save, keep-for what!!

I hate to tell you this, but I found out over in the
                                    Computer Science Department
that according to the latest statistics the death average is
                                    one hundred percent.
                    And you know, we are going to die,
                                    we're just going to die.
        I thought I'd leave you with that cheerful word—
                                    we're just gonna die.
You know, we want to
            save ourselves
                        and keep ourselves
                                    and hold ourselves back
as though the highest goal in life would be to look good
                                    in our caskets.
It's no special blessing to come to the end of life with
                                    love unshared
                                    selves ungiven
                            activities unactivated
                            deeds undone
                        emotions unextended.
            It's not an encouraging thought—
                especially at my age in life—
but I have the feeling that when
        a person is middle-aged
                he ought to be about half used-up.
                        And when I read this passage
                            I keep asking myself this question—
                    what am I saving myself for?
Isn't it God's intention that when we come to the end
                                    of the line
                            we're just about used up?
Sometime between now and then
we might as well be letting the candle burn
                        for the light
                        for the heat
                        for the warmth and sharing.
                        As long as we are going to live
                                    and then die
                    we'd just better live for Jesus
and love and go ahead and let ourselves be used up.

I think I need that at school.
                    A good friend of mine said,
"Teaching is a marvelous profession
                    if it weren't for the students."
About halfway through the fall quarter
        it might be good if you call me up
and remind me
of what I have written to you.
                            But I need to know—
                    what am I saving myself for?
                    He laid down his life for us—
                        we ought to lay down our lives
                        for the brethren.
As long as I can read that verse
        and say I'd be willing to die if I have to,
                I can go my way untouched
                        and unrebuked.
But when it says to me
                put it down brother—
                put your life down—
                then that meets me day by day
                        and challenges me
                            to decision and
                                discipleship.
And I think that is what the Holy Spirit
                has in mind for me and you.

The second word is just fantastic.
It is the Greek word that is translated "heart"
    and I have to write about it.
    It is not the word "kardia"
        from which we get words like cardiac.
        That is the normal Greek word for heart.
            The word here doesn't mean heart at all.
            It is "splangkna".
Isn't that a good word—
                your "splangknas".

See—   **"if anyone has the world's goods
and sees his brother in need
yet closes his splangknas against him
how does God's
love abide in
him?**

It's really interesting that the translators must have been
feeling very civilized
at the time this was translated
because what it really means
is "innards."
There is a real neat short word for it
that I hate to use in public.
Have you heard of "splangkna level" dialogue?
Maybe New Testament people didn't know too much
about physiology
but they sure did know a lot about people
and where you feel it
when you feel it.
When you have had your feelings hurt
where does it hurt?
And when you are heavy-hearted
where does the weight
rest?
Not in your heart,
but in your "splangknas"—that's where.
When there is tension and misunderstanding
in your home or at work
where does the dull heaviness rest?
In your innards—that's where.

Now here is the awesome
and wonderful thing about all this.

If we see our brother in need, yet close up our insides
                                 against him—
if it doesn't get to us
        if we keep aloof and cool
            and untouched and uninvolved
                if it doesn't get to us to tear up
                  our indigestion
                      at all—
                if we don't
                feel it
          where we really feel things—
        then-listen to this now—
      how does God's love abide in us?
Is St. John saying that the love of God is to be identified
  with the kind of love that we feel in our innards?
                Yes, he's saying that
           if you don't feel it there
      then how does God's love abide in you?
      Does that say anything to us
        about the way God loves?
             It says to us that God has
             opened up his insides to us.
             He has revealed His heart
             to us
                in Jesus Christ.
He is not impassive
        and aloof
        and untouched
        and uninvolved.
He has entered into the realities of our human lives at
                the feeling level.
          He has exposed himself
        and become utterly vulnerable—
          hanging out on a cross.
Then let's not love in word, but in truth.
        I think this is what John means when he says—
He laid down his life for us;
        and we ought to lay down our lives
            for the brethren.

I think we need to back away from these verses
and look at them in a more general way.
If we are to lay down our lives
and not hold them back—
if we are to love . . .
in deed and truth—
we need to know what kind of love it is
He lays on us.
What directions
does this love take?
How are we going to
work it out in practice?
I need to tell you,
if you don't know by now,
that I have a tendency to exaggerate
when I'm enthused.
And I am wanting to share with you some insights,
two or three things
that have indeed been life-changing
for me
in terms of what this love means.
And though I've talked about them
and thought about them to some degree
I haven't got them all integrated in yet,
so that if I were talking to you instead of writing
I'd probably yell once in awhile.

The first one is this:
in the teaching of First John
the love of which he speaks
is not so much directed toward God
as toward the brethren.
Let me give you a couple of scriptures.
He laid down his life for us
we ought to lay down our lives for the brethren.
(I John 3:16)

Herein is love,
  not that we loved God
  but that he loved us
    and sent His Son to be the expiation for your sins.
                Beloved, if God so loved us
                    we ought also
                        to love one another.
                        (I John 4:10,11)

Now you know,
  when you lay it out like that
  it is as clear as it can be
    but I cannot get over the fact
      of how revolutionary
        and radical
          that is.
      I think most of my life I was fetched up
            one way or another
        in the idea that we ought to love God;
                which,
            as you know,
               is true.
Let me tell you the first testimony you ever gave.
  Remember the very first testimony you ever gave?
             "I love the Lord
             and I want to go
             all the way with
                Him."
Where do you suppose that comes from?
    I don't know.
    But by now,
      I guess it is universal.
             "I love the Lord
             and I want to go
             all the way with
                Him."
And what I am seeing in First John is this—
  God is not so concerned that I love Him
    as that I believe He loves me
      and I love you.

You see we can get in a cycle here
God loves me
and I love God
and He loves me
and I love Him.
"Oh Lord I love thee,
I want to love Thee more,
more love to thee, O
Christ."
He laid down His life for me and so we sing,
"I'll live for Him who died for me."
And it is possible to get this
into a kind of cocoon
that withdraws us from the world
and from persons
in order to love God—
and that's not good.
I don't want to testify too much here
but I have to testify a little I suppose
because what I'm saying comes out of my life
and the Word as it has been meeting life.
But I remember—
I don't quite know how to say this
or if I ought to—
a long time ago
before I came to school
I had a lot more time to pray
and read the Bible
than I do now.
That may or may not be true,
but that's what I think.
There have been times in my life
when I spent more time alone
in solitude
and I prayed more than I do now.
Because when I moved to the college to teach—
and started teaching Greek every morning at 7:30
I mean I entered a whole new world.

And I found two things
  and it took awhile to get them together.
    I found I didn't have hardly any time at all
                  to myself.
  But I discovered that as
    I began to love people
      and to care for people
and become involved with people
  I had more joy
        more life
         more tears
           more laughter
             more meaning
and far greater fun and joy
  than I ever had before.
    Now don't misunderstand that,
I'm not saying we are not to get alone—
      we are.
But I don't think we are to withdraw
      and to say
          "O God I want to love Thee
                do I love Thee
              Lord I love Thee
           let me count the ways."
I think I'm beginning to believe
  that God is not as sentimental
    as we sometimes think He is.
I have weird mental images—
  there are some people
    in some churches that I remember
        and I remember one
        dear, poor, pitiful sister
          who used to stand up
    and say in a slow, whiny way,
      "Well, I love the Lord."
    And I could just see the Lord
      looking down and saying,
        "Oh, I'm so glad."

Do you think God has some giant, heavenly daisy,
                                   and He is saying
                              "He loves me
                                he loves me not
                                he loves me
                                he loves me not."
You should have been brought up in
        the church that I was brought up in—
           one of the blessings of it was
               that every odd character that ever lived
               had a prototype in that church
                   and I haven't met any strangers
                   since.
And I can remember a dear sister
        who used to get up and talk about
                              "Oh . . . I love the Lord."
She had her children all spread out on each side of her.
She'd sit back down and one of them would wiggle . .
                              "Ker-whump!"
                          You know . . .
                          "Mommy, can I . . ."

                          "Ker-whump!"
                      "I love the Lord . . ."
                          "Ker-whump!"
                              Well okay-
            and you know I am exaggerating,
                          but not too much.

It isn't God loves me and
        "Lord I need to love Thee more, yes
         help me to love Thee more,
            I do love Thee,
                       please help me to love Thee more.
                       Do I love Thee Lord,
                          yes, Lord I do love Thee."
            He laid down his life for us
    and we ought to lay down our lives for the brethren.
    Beloved, if God so loved us
        we ought also to love one another.

Now how about that?
That means that the flow of the love of God
is not to be back toward Him—

well, please understand;
that doesn't sound right,
but you know what I mean—

but love is to be out toward the brother.
Now maybe this is one of those radical things,
the continuity-discontinuity themes,
in which this love for the brother
is in fact, the thing which saves
and preserves
and expresses
our love for God.
It is in fact,
in the love for my brother
that the love of God
is guaranteed and perpetuated.
And it saves us from sentimentalism
and egotism
and self-centeredness
in all our holy ways
and words
and keeps us honest
and open
and real.

When you come right down to it,
how do I love God?
What do I have to give Him that He needs?
You know—
like Paul said in Romans—
"Who has given a gift to Him
that he might be repaid?"
For from Him
and through Him
and to Him are all things. (Romans 11:35,36)

How can I love Him?
Maybe the only way
that I can love God is by loving you.

Now if that is true
    that casts a whole new dimension
        on our living relationships with each other.
And I have to say this
that since I have had the privilege
            of living among the young
and the Bible study groups
    and the fellowships
        and the times of talking and sharing
            and laughing and crying
        and the impositions and the ecstasies—
you know,
the whole thing
that involves you
when you become a "people-people"—
as I have sought to express my trust in God's love for
me
                by deliberately
                    consciously loving persons—
                        I think I love God more
                                and better
                                and happier
                                than I ever did.
            And it doesn't come by withdrawing—
don't forget what we have been saying—
God has cast us into the world
    of the intricacies of inter-personal relationships
        and all this thing does hang together.
You see,
God is Trinity—Father, Son, Spirit.
The dynamics of the inner life of God
                is the dynamics of giving
                        and receiving
                        and loving.

Some have said that the Holy Spirit is the bond of love
between the Father and Son
and the bond of love
that reaches out to include all mankind
in that Holy fellowship;
so that our sharing of the experience of God in the power
of His Spirit is,
in fact,
an extension of the dynamic of love within God himself.
And the love of which He speaks
is not so much toward God
as toward the brother.
That is quite radical really,
and I think we'll all continue to say
"I love the Lord."
All right, but don't talk about loving the Lord
and not loving our brother—
somehow they go together
they belong together
you cannot separate them.
In fact,
"If a man loves God and hates his brother . . ."
that is,
if he says he loves God and hates his brother,
the Bible says
he's a liar.
That's pretty strong.
I really need to believe that God
is not so much concerned that I emote toward Him
as that I act in love toward you
and believe that He loves me.
I think that God is more concerned that I believe He
loves me
than that I love Him.
And that I express that trust in His love
by deliberately,
consciously
loving my brother.

And don't forget
    that "brother" means fellow Christian.
        Of course, we are to love
  all those who come into the circle of our world,
  but the place where love is to be going on
  is in the community of believers who share
  in the life of Christ.
If love is not going on between us who know the Lord,
        what good is talk about loving people
                "out there?"
      It doesn't mean anything anywhere
    if it doesn't mean anything here between us
            in the fellowship.
The Spirit won't let us generalize this too much.
        John is not talking about
        a spirit of good will
        toward mankind.
      He means love to real live people
  beginning with our Christian brothers and sisters
right here in the fellowship.

Here is another insight
      that has been changing me.
      It has come
    from hearing John say—
"When you say love think Jesus."
  It is not enough to say "God is love."
    The Bible doesn't end there.
You can take that statement by itself
  and make it a foundation stone—
    on which you can build
  just about any kind of religion you want.
  Christian Science is built on the idea "God is love."
    Buddhism
      Hinduism
        Universalism
          Humanitarianism
            can all be built on
                "God is love."

That's not a Christian statement standing alone.
Here's the Christian statement—
"God so loved the world He sent His Son
so that we might live through Him."
When the Bible says "God is love,"
it does not mean
God has a general benevolent feeling
toward mankind
and has opened many roads
toward which we may struggle to find Him.
It means that God has given Himself to us
in Jesus Christ.
The defining act
of the love of God is the coming of Jesus.
The word love needs a definition, doesn't it?
Jesus is the "lived out" word.
I read a beautiful thing once,
I wish I'd thought it myself.
I love to get good quotes
and never put down where I got them
until pretty soon
I think I thought them up
myself.
"The word love, needs a dictionary
and for Christians the dictionary is Jesus Christ.
He took that chameleon of a word
and gave it a fast color
so that ever since
it has lustered with His life and
teaching—
dyed in the crimson of Calvary
and shot through with the glories of
Easter morning."
Isn't that great?
That should be in the Bible
some scribe just missed it.

When we say love
   we can mean anything.
There are big words in Greek for love—
          "eros"
          "philos"
          "agape."
Eros is the love of desire—
      love of not only sex and lust—
   but love that seeks to own, to possess, to have.
A man says, "I just love oranges."
   If the orange could speak,
        it would say, "You don't love me—
          you just want to squeeze me!"
I love paintings
I love antiques
   or music
   or books—
   which mostly means I want to have them.
There's another level—philos,
from which we get words like
        Philadelphia—the city of brotherly love
   and fellowship.
   We have in common
     we give
       we receive
       we share.

              This is beautiful love
          and is God's precious gift to us
       but this is not the love
         that John is talking about.
       He is talking about
     love that thinks Jesus in the loving.
Agape love—
      which is not simply giving love,
         but giving love
           in the context of God's sending
             his son.

Now,
I don't want to run this in the ground
but
when you say love, think Jesus.
That's the Christian view.

By love
we do mean more
than a benevolent spirit toward mankind.
That makes me
think of another
good quote I
read somewhere.

"It's a shame that in the minds
of so many, the Christian
religion has been identified
with pious ethical behavior
together with a vague belief
in God suffused with aesthetic
emotionalism and a mild
glow of humanitarian
benevolence."

Isn't that great?
Or perhaps awful.

That makes you think
of a nice pastor
in a nice church
preaching a nice sermon
to a nice congregation
telling them to be nicer—
"the bland leading the bland".

That is not
what the New Testament means by love.
Love is a strong word.
It does not mean total tolerance
or universalism.
It means that when we say love—
we are thinking of Jesus.

We are sharing His love—
                    not mutuality
                    not congeniality
                    not what you have
                    in real neat service clubs
         plus the inspiration of the Holy Spirit
                    not mutual affection
                    plus blessing.
It expresses itself
  in that love that comes
      from Jesus Christ.

What is it that makes it possible for people to
  have long, enduring
    deepening, close, affectionate
      friendships
    without growing sordid
    without wife-swapping
    without it becoming unclean
              and adulterated?
I know we have our troubles and every so often
                            somebody
                  runs off with the wrong
                      somebody.
But what is it that makes it possible
  for couples
    and families
      and friends
        to love each other
          reach out to each other
          and touch each other
                for years
                    and years
                    and years
without its becoming unclean or sordid—
                not denying chemistries
                  or vibrations
                  or potentials,
              not denying temptations
                  or possibilities?

How can we be friends
for long periods of time
and it still be good
and wholesome
and rich
and beautiful
and supportive?
Because the love of Jesus
strengthens us.
Something very precious happens
when we say in Jesus
"I love you."
His love is always healing, cleansing
lifting, preserving.
It is a good word—
because Jesus gave it a fast color.

Here is another life-changing insight for me
that is both old and new.
Love is commanded.
Some things cannot be commanded
and we think love is one of them.
But right here it says just as plain as day—
And this commandment we have from him
that he who loves God
should love his brother also.
(1 John 4:21)

We are commanded
to love
one another.
You see,
it has to move suddenly
out of the realm of attraction.
There are some people
that we like
and then there are the other kind.
And some who like us
and some we can't understand.

Now look,
if Christian love is restricted to those we have
                                    natural, warm feeling for
                  we have limited our world
                        to the little group we happen to be
                                                  around.

        But,
love is commanded
        and if we are going to talk about love
                we have to move out of the level of
                        liking
                          and emotion
                            and feeling
                              and warmth
                                to the level of the will—
                                      a posture
                                      a stance
                                      an attitude
                                    a frame of mind
                          a life's direction toward others
                  that's conditioned by our understanding
                                            of God's
                                    self-giving in Jesus.
              We are commanded.
              It isn't as though
                      we had any
                          alternative.
                  Have we accepted that yet,
                          do you suppose?

I think it is time to get more practical—
    and maybe time for a word of review.
                              We have been saying
                            that the life of God
                          that Jesus brings into our world
                      is a shared life.
                      God's love for us that "comes down"—
                                    the vertical line—
is to be expressed out through the
    horizontal line of our personal relationships.

God's love for us is defined
  by the giving of His Son, Jesus,
and love for each other
  is defined by Him, too.
Our love for each other behaves like Jesus.

Let me try to put some handles
  on all this talk about love
    to help us pull it down
      into the flow of daily life.
I'm sure that what I'm going to say now
                    is in First John somewhere.
                    You may have to look
                        between the lines
                    and in the margins—
                    but surely it is there.

Love that behaves like Jesus
        means care for persons
            as persons.
              We are to see persons in a personal way,
                    not in a "thingy" way.
We have a tendency to put people into categories—
              that's "thingy"
              that "thingizes" them—
                it turns them into "its" instead of
                                "yous".
  You know how Southerners are.
  I do 'cause I'm not one.
  You know how Westerners are,
                  you know how the Mexicans
                      the Blacks
                        the Orientals are.
                  Put them into categories,
                  slip them into little slots
                        categorized
                        depersonalized
                  massed-up
                    and that's not love.
                  Love sees the person.

I never will forget one afternoon
     when I was coming back from a retreat
        up in the Sierras.
              I was taking the back way home
and there were
about four or five cars coming down the mountains.
          It was back of Fresno
          out in the hot valley
          and it was about 110°
          and we took a kind of a back road
          and they were doing repair work on it.
And we were just cruising along there and a patrolman
                    pulled us over.
Five of us—and it was just dumb.
Here we were 50 miles from nowhere—
     five irate drivers and this young cop.
There we stood in the boiling sun
     mad as could be
              at the injustice of the whole thing.
              And right in the midst
              of all my disgust I
              looked at this young
              patrolman—and he was young—
and he was writing out tickets to five angry drivers
          and he was trembling.
          That was one of my better days.
He was writing with nervous hands
     and the creases of his pants were just shaking.
          And suddenly my whole attitude changed—
not that he was right—
    but it meant my whole relationship to him changed
      because suddenly I saw him as a young policeman
          nervous as could be, wanting to do it right
             and probably wishing to goodness
                he could have let us go.
        But there he was—
            caught
            and trembling
            and nervous
            and suddenly I knew how he felt.

Behind the uniform was a real,
                    live people.
          It's kind of an awesome thing,
                         isn't it?
     Suddenly my own guilts are rising,
we all know those people who fade into the furniture—
                         you know,
                    you don't hear them
                    you don't see them
                    you don't know they are there.
          But I've learned a few things the hard way—
                    and one of them is
          that there isn't anybody who is a nobody.
          Everybody is a somebody
                         and
          everybody is a "real live people"—
with real hopes
     and real dreams
          and fears
               and longings
                    and desires.

I've learned a few things about myself lately.
     I'm really very sensitive.
                    It took me a long time to accept that.
But I am—
     I'm sensitive as I can be.
     I think I might make a good pastor
          if there weren't any such things as votes.
          I "loves" them contracts.
               And I can't stand votes—
                    I think they're of the devil.
                    But I know I'm sensitive
               and I'm probably half neurotic about it.
And on the heels of that newfound knowledge
  has come another fascinating discovery—
     everybody is sensitive,
          there isn't anybody who's not sensitive.

"Oh you know so and so—you couldn't hurt him.
It runs like water off a duck's back."
   Oh no it doesn't.
   Did you know that—
      skinny people are sensitive
      that fat people are sensitive
     that hairy people are sensitive
     that bald people are sensitive
     and tall people are sensitive
    and short people are sensitive?
      Everybody is sensitive.
      Love says I care for you
          as a person.
Love says in word and response I see you
       I hear you
       I know you are there.
   I am aware of *you*—
       I see *you*
       I hear *you*
       I know *you* are there.
That's almost so simple as to be ridiculous.
But nothing has made more impression on me
      than just that very thing.
I went to a big church convention one time
and it was just like I knew it was going to be.
        You know,
      here's this thingy on you,
and you meet somebody and he looks at your badge
        and says,
    "Hi, how are you?"
Then before you can answer
  he's looking over your shoulder
     for somebody better than you to talk to.
And so you spend a week bumping into people—
    never having time to talk to anybody
    and nobody ever really looks at you.
"Oh, hi, how are you?"
and you're on your way.
I don't know who everybody was looking for
  but everybody was more important than I was.

And then sure as the world,
    some guy you don't especially want to see
      will just glue in on you.
         But love says
           I see you.
              Just like that—
              I *see you.*

Here's a little thing—
do you want a handle for all this?
      Love says look at the people you're talking to.
                Just look at them—
                    go ahead—
                    look at them.
         Don't look up there at the ceiling
              don't look over there
       don't put your hands in your pockets
             or draw on the ground.
        Don't kick the tire just look at them.
                      I see you.

I remember not too long ago—
      not long enough ago—
I was sitting in the living room reading
and my daughter, Susan, said, "Daddy,
             Daddy—
                Daddy."
And Mary Jo, her mother, said, "Why don't you,
         just for fun, count up the times
    you have to say "Daddy" before he answers?"
      Now I heard that
        and it didn't bless me a whole lot.
I think the thing that hurt the most was
    that I'm not that kind of person.
You know—I'm the warm,
           friendly,
         caring,
           outgoing type—
             I tell people that
             everywhere I go.

I'm that type of person.
But here I was reading a book—
actually it testifies to my
fantastic powers of concentration—
and if that day at school was a normal day at school
I had listened
            and talked
                and shared
                    with five or six students
and I came home and was sitting in my living room
    reading a book and my very own daughter
        who is very precious to me
            was saying to me, "Daddy,
                        Daddy—
                                Daddy."
                    That's not too good, is it?
Love says
        I'll put the paper down,
        I'll turn the knob off,
        I will look
        and I will listen
        and all of me is present here
                        to listen and
                            to look at you.

When I go home after spending a weekend
                        speaking at a retreat or something,
        if it has been a normal weekend at home—
            you know—I've been gone,
                    I've been wined and dined,
                    I've had some good fellowship,
                        I've had some solitude—
        it's about time for the dishwasher to go out
    or the radiator hose to break
    or the battery to go down
    or some other dumb thing.
Or the favorite trick—that being the bank balance
                        getting all fouled up.

You see,
  I go back home to my wife
  and she has been father,
                 mother,
                   and mostly chauffeur,
                     and life has gone around and around—
and I come back all filled up with what I've been doing
  and she's all filled up with what she's been doing
    and since I'm the one who's talking about love
      guess who ends up listening.
Here's the way it ought to be.
                I'm not testifying just
              telling you how it ought to be.
When I go home, she'll say to me,
    "How did it go?"
And I ought to say,
        "Fantastic. I wish you had been there.
        How did your weekend go?"
And then I need to just be quiet for half an hour or more
                  and just listen.
                      You see,
      her words can come into my ears
           while I'm looking around
      waiting to tell her about this and that.
But I need to just lay my words aside and look
                   and listen
      and bring all of my attention to her—
               as a person.
Isn't that what love means?
All of me is here—
  at attention
  to care,
    and to will your good.
It is really interesting that half the people
      who come into my office—
        well, more than that but I hate to admit it—
        begin our conversations by saying—
"Now I know you don't have any answers for me"—
        which helps my ego tremendously.

But really what people need from me is not answers—
but a real
live person
listening
and caring.
That's what love means—
I see you
I hear you
I know you are there.
Listen to your husband—
look at him.
Listen to your wife—
look at her.
Listen to your children—
look at them.
What if we really listened—
what if we really looked—
what if we really saw each other?

When I was a child we lived way out in the country,
way out in the San Joaquin Valley in central California.
It was fifteen miles to Delano
where we went to school
and twenty-five miles another way
to Porterville,
where we went to church
and in the other direction
there wasn't anything
but the foothills of the Sierras.
If you came to see us,
you came to see us—
because nobody ever was just passin' by.
We lived so far
out in the country
that when the Electrolux man came
we had him stay for supper.
My father was a quiet man
but I can remember when people would drive
all the way from town
just to talk to him.

And I can remember times
when people would come out
and I could hear the feeling and emotion
but not always the words they were
saying to Dad,
and my Dad would be
saying stuff like "Hm-m.
Well, my, my.
Well, isn't that a sight.
Hmph, yes sir."
Then after awhile
the fellow would say—
"Well, Mr. Welch,
I sure do thank you for your help."
And he'd get in his car
and ride the twenty miles back home
and my father had said,
"Hmph, now isn't that a sight."
I'll tell you something—
twenty miles
is not too far to go
to talk to someone who will listen
and care
and look
and understand
and hear
even if all he says is
"Well, what do you know."
That's true, isn't it?
I'm getting guilty
about how little I really listen—
let's talk about
another handle
we can put on love.

Love says I release you
        and will not judge you.
        I'm not sure that writing about this
            will help my guilt any—
          this is a hard one.
I wish I'd written about it when my children were little.
    I could have released them then
  when they were too dependent to be released.
It's much harder now that they are getting independent.
                But we don't own each other.
               I don't own my children,
               I don't own my wife.
Our ultimate ties
        are ties of love
           that must be freely given.
              I am commanded to love
                  but not to own
                     or control
                     or dominate.

      Every once in a while
    I need to engage in a little mental exercise
that puts my family up on a large pedestal
             about six feet high.
    I walk around the pedestal and look them over,
             one by one, and say,
           "I love you
           I release you.
      I am responsible to you
            and for you—
           but I do not own you.
I will not force you to find your fulfillment
              in my fulfillment—
      but I'll let you go
    to be your own person
  and find your own fulfillment
      supported by my love and care."
How easy to write about this exercise
    and how hard to do it.

It is a wonderful experience
  to be with college students—
  to be about the age of their parents
      and not be a parent,
  to be a father figure to some of them
      and not be a father.
Though I'm not really a father figure
  because I'm too young.
I love them
    and care very much about them
    but I do not own them
 and cannot control what they do
nor act as judge over what they do.
    I have no alternative—
    I must release them.
And the marvelous
  happy
  surprising thing is this:
     persons change
     in the atmosphere
     of releasing,
      unjudging love!
I don't mean that it's a refined, Christian way
 of getting people to do what you want them to—
but caring
 releasing
 unjudging love
    deliberately given in the love of Jesus
    becomes the agent for beautiful change
      in a person's life.

    But oh, the spirit of judgment.
Do you know how to be happy with a group of people
      for a long time?
      Don't judge.
 A spirit of judgment will kill the honeymoon.

That's precisely the point
    that brings about the old proverb—
        if you can keep the young
          converts
      away from the old saints
      long enough to get established
      you'll be alright—
because the old saints have been touched
       with a spirit of cynicism
           and judgment.
Someone new comes into the church
    and says, "Isn't the pastor marvelous"
      and "Isn't the choir fantastic"
      and I can just hear the old saint—
        "Dearie, you just wait around
           awhile—you'll see."
That's true, isn't it?
It's not right
    but it's true.
To the newcomer
      it's just heaven on earth
      in the community,
but let them hang around awhile and our cynicism
           will get them.
        It's catching, isn't it?
        It's the plague.

You would not believe some of the letters
    that students show me from their parents.
    And parents wouldn't believe
      that students show them to me, either.
I read letters that say in all kinds of ways—
      "I don't trust you
        you aren't good
      when will you ever change
    you are always late, why don't you write
      you aren't responsible
      you are a disappointment
after all we've done for you,
      you'll have to get married—
        you'll get pregnant."

I have seen the long arm of parental control
                                        and judgment
    reach across the miles from home to dormitory
and almost destroy the precious
                                growing, seeking life
                        of a young college student.
If I were speaking in public
    I think I would be yelling about now.
        That deadly spirit of judgment is indeed the plague.
But love,
        Jesus' kind of love,
        has the releasing
                affirming power to stay the plague
                                        and heal our lives.
        What a handle—
                I love you
                I release you
                I will not judge you.
We really do need each other.
All this talk about love is not something ethereal
                                        and distant.
        It has handles that reach right down to where we are.
Let's pray a moment together.

Lord Jesus, help us to learn to show love.
        Help us to take time to listen
                to give our attention to the ones around us
                to be more aware of the sensitivities of others.
        Help us to see people as people—
        as real live people
                with feelings and concerns
                that are just like ours.
Help us Lord not to judge
    and help us not to allow our cynicism
        to deprive others of joy.
            Teach us Lord, to love
                In deed and in spirit.
                    Amen.

Chapter Five

WE REALLY DO NEED
EACH OTHER

Let me just tell you this true thing before
   I stop writing.
At school a few years ago
there was a summer school course in "Group and
                                  Interpersonal
                                  Relations."
   About a dozen people took the class
   and at the end of it
      they decided they wanted to do something
                           together
                  as kind of closing to the class.
                  You know,
               they had come to know each other,
                     and to share each other,
            and really be personal to each other
                     and break down walls
                     and so forth—
so they decided to get together and take a hike
                        up to Hennigar Flats.
Now, Hennigar Flats is about three miles
      up the side of the mountain behind the campus
      and it takes about an hour and a half
         for anyone to make the hike.

So they set the day
> and made the sandwiches
> and made the chocolate
> and brought the cold drinks
> and the back packs
> and they got all gathered up
>> for the safari
> and they started up the mountain—
>> together.

But it wasn't long until
the strong, stalwart ones were up in front and
the other ones were back in the middle and
> way back at the end of the line
>> was a girl named Jane—
> who was, you might say,
>> out of shape.

At the front was Don—
> a big, strong, former paratrooper.
He and some others—the strong ones—
> were up in front and
the weak ones were back in the back and
> way in the back
>> was Jane.
>> And Don said—
>> it was he who told me the story—
> he looked back a couple of switchbacks
>> and saw Jane

> and the Lord told him
> that he had just better go back
> and walk with her.
That's kind of hard on him because he has a need to be
>> *first.*
But he went down
> and started walking with Jane
> and the people in the level above called down,
>> "Come on up.
>> It's great up here."
>> And Jane yelled, "I don't think I can
>>> make it."

And they hollered, "Yeah, you can.
Try harder, come on up."
And every time they called to her
down went her own sense of worth
down went her own sense of value—
"I can't make it."
"Oh, yeah, you can. Come on."

So the strong went on ahead
and the weak hung behind
and here was Jane
and she never made it to the top.

Now, look what you have.
You have a group—
we know each other
we like each other
we want to do this together
let's go to Hennigar Flats together.
But before long, you have divided
the strong and the weak
the haves and the have-nots
and the ables and the unables.
So what started out as a group
has now become a fragmented collection.
And so the strong say,
"You can do it."
And the weak say,
"No, I can't."
And so the strong say
"Try harder"—
which is a big help.
That's a big help.
And she didn't make it.
Thankfully, that's not the last chapter.
They must have learned their lessons
because they decided that was no way
to end the fellowship of that class
and they got together and decided
to do it again.

But they made some new rules—
it was everybody go
or nobody go
and they were all going
together.
So they set the day
and made the sandwiches
and made the chocolate
and brought the cold drinks
and the back packs
and they got all gathered up
for the safari,
and they started up the mountain.
It took them four hours to make it to the top,
and the water was all gone
and the cold drinks were all gone
and the sandwiches were all gone
and the chocolate was all gone
and the back packs were empty
but they all made it,
together.

Let me share with you
the thing that this real life parable
has been saying to me—
we have got to go together.
Christian fellowship is no place
for get in or get out—
it's get in,
get in.
And if you need to slow down—
you slow down.
That's why it's good for us to read scripture
and sing hymns together—
the slow folks have to speed up
and the fast folks have to slow down
and we have to do it together.
I know, don't you,
that it is God's intention
that we go together as a body.

It doesn't help much for those who have made it
  to say to us weaklings—
        "Try harder.
         See, I've done it,
           so you can make it."
That makes me think of some dear old grandmother
  whose children are all gone,
    who spends all day praying
      and listening to holy records,
saying to a young mother
  going out of her mind
    with little kids and noise—
                "Oh, honey, just get
                  alone with God."
               Yeah, thanks a lot.
           You can't even get alone
          in the bathroom anymore.

You know something—
we're all just people who need each other.
We're all learning
  and we've all got a long journey ahead of us.
      We've got to go together
          and if it takes us until Jesus comes
      we better stay together
      we better help each other.
And I dare say
  that by the time we get there
    all the sandwiches will be gone
  and all the chocolate will be gone
  and all the water will be gone
  and all the backpacks will be empty.
But no matter how long it takes us
      we've got to go together.
      Because that's how it is
        in the body of Christ.

It's all of us
  in love
    in care
      in support
        in mutuality—
          we really do need each other.
          Let's pray.

Oh, Lord Jesus,
  bring us together,
  keep us together
         seeing,
           hearing,
             aware,
               sensitive.
           We need to look at our children
       and listen to our parents
      and be sensitive to each other
    and aware of each other.
      Teach us to know that it's Thy will
        that we go together.
      Teach us to know that it's not
        our mutualities
        and congenialities
        that bind us—
     it's the life of Jesus Christ
       that binds us—
    and so we belong together
        and we must go together.
          Amen.